The Warrior's Bible

Compiled by Whitman Berry

**TWO OCEANS
PUBLISHING**

2016

**TWO OCEANS
PUBLISHING**

Published by Two Oceans Publishing

PO Box 1718
West Perth
WA 6872
Australia

ISBN 978-0-9945178-3-8

www.TwoOceansPublishing.com.au

The Warrior's Bible

In the beginning God created the
heaven and the earth.

Genesis 1.01

✝

And God saw the light, that it
was good: and God divided the
light from the darkness.

Genesis 1.04

✝

And God said, Let us make man in
our image, after our likeness: and let them
have dominion over the fish of the sea, and
over the fowl of the air, and over the cattle,
and over all the earth, and over every creeping
thing that creepeth upon the earth.

Genesis 1.26

✝

So God created man in his own image,
in the image of God created he him; male and
female created he them.

Genesis 1.27

Therefore shall a man leave his father and his mother, and shall cleave unto his wife: and they shall be one flesh.

Genesis 2.24

✠

And the Lord said, My spirit shall not always strive with man, for that he also is flesh: yet his days shall be an hundred and twenty years.

Genesis 6.03

✠

And God saw that the wickedness of man was great in the earth, and that every imagination of the thoughts of his heart was only evil continually.

Genesis 6.05

✠

And it repented the Lord that he had made man on the earth, and it grieved him at his heart.

Genesis 6.06

The earth also was corrupt before God, and
the earth was filled with violence.

Genesis 6.11

✠

Whoso sheddeth man's blood, by man
shall his blood be shed: for in the image
of God made he man.

Genesis 9.06

✠

And I will make of thee a great nation,
and I will bless thee, and make thy name
great; and thou shalt be a blessing.

Genesis 12.02

✠

And the vale of Siddim was full of
slimepits; and the kings of Sodom and
Gomorrah fled, and fell there; and they
that remained fled to the mountain.

Genesis 14.01

And they took all the goods of Sodom and
Gomorrah, and all their victuals,
and went their way.

Genesis 14.11

✞

And when Abram heard that his brother was
taken captive, he armed his trained servants,
born in his own house, three hundred and
eighteen, and pursued them unto Dan.

Genesis 14.14

✞

And he divided himself against them, he
and his servants, by night, and smote them,
and pursued them unto Hobah, which is on
the left hand of Damascus.

Genesis 14.15

✞

And he brought back all the goods, and also
brought again his brother Lot, and his goods,
and the women also, and the people.

Genesis 14.16

And the angel of the Lord said unto her,
Behold, thou art with child and shalt bear a son,
and shalt call his name Ishmael; because the
Lord hath heard thy affliction.

Genesis 16.11

✝

And he will be a wild man; his hand will
be against every man, and every man's hand
against him; and he shall dwell in the
presence of all his brethren.

Genesis 16.12

✝

Then the Lord rained upon Sodom and
upon Gomorrah brimstone and fire from
the Lord out of heaven;

Genesis 19.24

✝

And he overthrew those cities, and all the
plain, and all the inhabitants of the cities, and
that which grew upon the ground.

Genesis 19.25

Now therefore take, I pray thee, thy weapons,
thy quiver and thy bow, and go out to the field,
and take me some venison.

Genesis 27.03

✠

And God said unto him, I am God Almighty:
be fruitful and multiply; a nation and a company
of nations shall be of thee, and kings shall come
out of thy loins.

Genesis 35.11

✠

The archers have sorely grieved him, and
shot at him, and hated him.

Genesis 49.23

✠

But his bow abode in strength, and the arms
of his hands were made strong by the hands of
the mighty God of Jacob; (from thence is the
shepherd, the stone of Israel).

Genesis 49.24

And the Lord said, I have surely seen
the affliction of my people which are in Egypt,
and have heard their cry by reason of their
taskmasters; for I know their sorrows.

Exodus 3.07

✝

And I am come down to deliver them out
of the hand of the Egyptians, and to bring them
up out of that land unto a good land and a large,
unto a land flowing with milk and honey . . .

Exodus 3.08

✝

. . . at midnight the Lord smote all the firstborn in
the land of Egypt, from the firstborn of Pharaoh that
sat on his throne unto the firstborn of the captive that
was in the dungeon; and all the firstborn of cattle.

Exodus 12.29

✝

The Lord shall fight for you, and ye shall
hold your peace.

Exodus 14.14

And the Lord said unto Moses, Stretch out thine hand over the sea, that the waters may come again upon the Egyptians, upon their chariots, and upon their horsemen.

Exodus 14.26

✝

And Moses stretched forth his hand over the sea, and the sea returned to his strength when the morning appeared; and the Egyptians fled against it; and the Lord overthrew the Egyptians in the midst of the sea.

Exodus 14.27

✝

And the waters returned, and covered the chariots and horsemen, and all the host of Pharaoh that came into the sea; there remained not so much as one of them.

Exodus 14.28

✝

But the children of Israel walked upon dry land in the midst of the sea; and the waters were a wall unto them on their right hand, and on their left.

Exodus 14.29

Thus the Lord saved Israel that day out of the hand of the Egyptians; and Israel saw the Egyptians dead upon the sea shore.

Exodus 14.30

✠

The Lord is my strength and song, and he is become my salvation: he is my God, and I will prepare him an habitation; my father's God, and I will exalt him.

Exodus 15.02

✠

The Lord is a man of war: the Lord is his name.

Exodus 15.03

✠

Thy right hand, O Lord, is become glorious in power: thy right hand, O Lord, hath dashed in pieces the enemy.

Exodus 15.06

And in the greatness of thine excellency
thou hast overthrown them that rose up against
thee: thou sentest forth thy wrath, which
consumed them as stubble.

Exodus 15.07

✟

Thou in thy mercy hast led forth the people
which thou hast redeemed: thou hast guided
them in thy strength unto thy holy
habitation.

Exodus 15.13

✟

The Lord shall reign for ever and ever.

Exodus 15.18

✟

And Joshua discomfited Amalek and his
people with the edge of the sword.

Exodus 17.13

Eye for eye, tooth for tooth,
hand for hand, foot for foot,

Exodus 21.24

✠

Burning for burning, wound for wound,
stripe for stripe.

Exodus 21.25

✠

Thou shalt not suffer a witch to live.

Exodus 22.18

✠

Whosoever lieth with a beast shall
surely be put to death.

Exodus 22.19

✠

He that sacrificeth unto any god, save unto the
Lord only, he shall be utterly destroyed.

Exodus 22.20

And my wrath shall wax hot, and I will kill
you with the sword; and your wives shall
be widows, and your children fatherless.

Exodus 22.24

✠

Keep thee far from a false matter; and the
innocent and righteous slay thou not: for
I will not justify the wicked.

Exodus 23.07

✠

Take heed to thyself, lest thou make a covenant
with the inhabitants of the land whither thou goest,
lest it be for a snare in the midst of thee:

Exodus 34.12

✠

But ye shall destroy their altars, break their
images, and cut down their groves:

Exodus 34.13

✠

For thou shalt worship no other god: for the Lord, whose name is Jealous, is a jealous God.

Exodus 34.14

✠

If a man also lie with mankind, as he lieth with a woman, both of them have committed an abomination: they shall surely be put to death; their blood shall be upon them.

Leviticus 20.13

✠

And he that blasphemeth the name of the Lord, he shall surely be put to death, and all the congregation shall certainly stone him: as well the stranger, as he that is born in the land, when he blasphemeth the name of the Lord, shall be put to death.

Leviticus 20.16

✠

And he that killeth any man shall surely be put to death.

Leviticus 24.17

And he that killeth a beast shall make
it good; beast for beast.

Leviticus 24.18

✝

And if a man cause a blemish in his neighbour;
as he hath done, so shall it be done to him;

Leviticus 24.19

✝

Breach for breach, eye for eye, tooth for tooth:
as he hath caused a blemish in a man, so
shall it be done to him again.

Leviticus 24.20

✝

And he that killeth a beast, he shall restore it:
and he that killeth a man, he shall be
put to death.

Leviticus 24.21

✝

Ye shall have one manner of law, as well for the stranger, as for one of your own country: for I am the Lord your God.

Leviticus 24.22

✛

If ye walk in my statutes, and keep my commandments, and do them;

Leviticus 26.03

✛

Then I will give you rain in due season, and the land shall yield her increase, and the trees of the field shall yield their fruit.

Leviticus 26.04

✛

And your threshing shall reach unto the vintage, and the vintage shall reach unto the sowing time: and ye shall eat your bread to the full, and dwell in your land safely.

Leviticus 26.05

And I will give peace in the land, and ye shall
lie down, and none shall make you afraid: and
I will rid evil beasts out of the land, neither
shall the sword go through your land.

Leviticus 26.06

✞

And ye shall chase your enemies, and they
shall fall before you by the sword.

Leviticus 26.07

✞

Five of you shall chase an hundred, and an hundred
of you shall put ten thousand to flight: and your
enemies shall fall before you by the sword.

Leviticus 26.08

✞

And if ye go to war in your land against the enemy
that oppresseth you, then ye shall blow an alarm
with the trumpets; and ye shall be remembered
before the Lord your God, and ye shall be saved
from your enemies.

Numbers 10.09

And they turned and went up by the way of Bashan:
and Og the king of Bashan went out against them,
he, and all his people, to the battle at Edrei.

Numbers 21.33

✟

And the Lord said unto Moses, fear him not: for
I have delivered him into thy hand, and all his
people . . . do to him as thou didst unto Sihon king
of the Amorites, which dwelt at Heshbon.

Numbers 21.34

✟

So they smote him, and his sons, and all his
people, until there was none left him alive: and
they possessed his land.

Numbers 21.35

✟

I shall see him, but not now: I shall behold him, but
not nigh: there shall come a Star out of Jacob, and a
Sceptre shall rise out of Israel, and shall smite the
corners of Moab and destroy all children of Sheth.

Numbers 24.17

Then ye shall drive out all the inhabitants of the land from before you, and destroy all their pictures, and destroy all their molten images, and quite pluck down all their high places.

Numbers 33.52

✟

And ye shall dispossess the inhabitants of the land, and dwell therein: for I have given you the land to possess it.

Numbers 33.53

✟

This day will I begin to put the dread of thee and the fear of thee upon the nations that are under the whole heaven, who shall hear report of thee, and shall tremble, and be in anguish because of thee.

Deuteronomy 2.25

✟

Then Sihon came out against us, he and all his people, to fight at Jahaz.

Deuteronomy 2.32

And the Lord our God delivered him before us; and we smote him, and his sons, and all his people.

Deuteronomy 2.33

✤

And we took all his cities at that time, and utterly destroyed the men, and the women, and the little ones, of every city, we left none to remain.

Deuteronomy 2.34

✤

From Aroer, which is by the brink of the river of Arnon, and from the city that is by the river, even unto Gilead, there was not one city too strong for us: the Lord our God delivered all unto us.

Deuteronomy 2.36

✤

Then we turned, and went up the way to Bashan: and Og the king of Bashan came out against us, he and all his people, to battle at Edrei.

Deuteronomy 3.01

And the Lord said unto me, Fear him not: for I will deliver him, and all his people, and his land, into thy hand; and thou shalt do unto him as thou didst unto Sihon king of the Amorites, which dwelt at Heshbon.

Deuteronomy 3.02

✝

So the Lord our God delivered into our hands Og also, the king of Bashan, and all his people: and we smote him until none was left to him remaining.

Deuteronomy 3.03

✝

And we took all his cities at that time, there was not a city which we took not from them, threescore cities, all the region of Argob, the kingdom of Og in Bashan.

Deuteronomy 3.04

✝

All these cities were fenced with high walls, gates, and bars; beside unwalled towns a great many.

Deuteronomy 3.05

And we utterly destroyed them, as we did unto
Sihon king of Heshbon, utterly destroying the
men, women, and children, of every city.

Deuteronomy 3.06

✝

Ye shall not fear them: for the Lord your
God he shall fight for you.

Deuteronomy 3.22

✝

And when the Lord thy God shall deliver them
before thee; thou shalt smite them, and utterly
destroy them; thou shalt make no covenant with
them, nor shew mercy unto them.

Deuteronomy 7.02

✝

For thou art an holy people unto the Lord thy
God: the Lord thy God hath chosen thee to be
a special people unto himself, above all people
that are upon the face of the earth.

Deuteronomy 7.06

And the Lord thy God will put out those nations before thee by little and little: thou mayest not consume them at once, lest the beasts of the field increase upon thee.

Deuteronomy 7.22

✝

But the Lord thy God shall deliver them unto thee, and shall destroy them with a mighty destruction, until they be destroyed.

Deuteronomy 7.23

✝

And he shall deliver their kings into thine hand, and thou shalt destroy their name from under heaven: there shall no man be able to stand before thee, until thou have destroyed them.

Deuteronomy 7.24

✝

Let me alone, that I may destroy them, and blot out their name from under heaven: and I will make of thee a nation mightier and greater than they.

Deuteronomy 9.14

There shall no man be able to stand before you:
for the Lord your God shall lay the fear of you
and the dread of you upon all the land that ye
shall tread upon, as he hath said unto you.

Deuteronomy 11.25

✝

Thou shalt surely smite the inhabitants of that
city with the edge of the sword, destroying it
utterly, and all that is therein, and the cattle
thereof, with the edge of the sword.

Deuteronomy 13.15

✝

When thou goest out to battle against thine
enemies, and seest horses, and chariots, and a
people more than thou, be not afraid of them:
for the Lord thy God is with thee . . .

Deuteronomy 20.01

✝

. . . when ye are come nigh unto the battle, the
priest shall approach and speak unto the people.

Deuteronomy 20.02

And shall say unto them, Hear, O Israel, ye approach this day unto battle against your enemies: let not your hearts faint, fear not, and do not tremble, neither be ye terrified because of them.

Deuteronomy 20.03

✝

For the Lord your God is he that goeth with you, to fight for you against your enemies, to save you.

Deuteronomy 20.04

✝

And when the Lord thy God hath delivered it into thine hands, thou shalt smite every male thereof with the edge of the sword.

Deuteronomy 20.13

✝

But the women, and the little ones, and the cattle, and all that is in the city, even all the spoil thereof, shalt thou take unto thyself; and thou shalt eat the spoil of thine enemies, which the Lord thy God hath given thee.

Deuteronomy 20.14

Thus shalt thou do unto all the cities which are very far off from thee, which are not of the cities of these nations.

Deuteronomy 20.15

✠

But of the cities of these people, which the Lord thy God doth give thee for an inheritance, thou shalt save alive nothing that breatheth.

Deuteronomy 20.16

✠

When thou shalt besiege a city a long time, in making war against it to take it, thou shalt not destroy the trees thereof by forcing an axe against them: for thou mayest eat of them, and thou shalt not cut them down to employ them in the siege.

Deuteronomy 20.19

✠

When thou goest forth to war against thine enemies, and the Lord thy God hath delivered them into thine hands, and thou hast taken them captive.

Deuteronomy 21.10

And seest among the captives a beautiful woman, and hast a desire unto her, that thou wouldest have her to thy wife;

Deuteronomy 21.11

✟

Then thou shalt bring her home to thine house, and she shall shave her head, and pare her nails;

Deuteronomy 21.12

✟

And she shall put the raiment of her captivity from off her, and shall remain in thine house, and bewail her father and her mother a full month: and after that thou shalt go in unto her, and be her husband, and she shall be thy wife.

Deuteronomy 21.13

✟

And it shall be, if thou have no delight in her, then thou shalt let her go whither she will; but thou shalt not sell her at all for money, thou shalt not make merchandise of her, because thou hast humbled her.

Deuteronomy 21.14

He that is wounded in the stones, or hath his privy member cut off, shall not enter into the congregation of the Lord.

Deuteronomy 23.01

✝

The fathers shall not be put to death for the children, neither shall the children be put to death for the fathers: every man shall be put to death for his own sin.

Deuteronomy 24.16

✝

Cursed be he that taketh reward to slay an innocent person. And all the people shall say, Amen.

Deuteronomy 27.25

✝

Be strong and of a good courage, fear not, nor be afraid of them: for the Lord thy God, he it is that doth go with thee; he will not fail thee, nor forsake thee.

Deuteronomy 31.06

I will make mine arrows drunk with blood, and my sword shall devour flesh; and that with the blood of the slain and of the captives, from the beginning of revenges upon the enemy.

Deuteronomy 32.42

✝

So the people shouted when the priests blew the trumpets: and when the people heard the trumpets and gave a great shout, the wall fell down flat, so the people went into the city . . . and took the city.

Joshua 6.20

✝

And they utterly destroyed all that was in the city, both man and woman, young and old, and ox, and sheep, and ass, with the edge of the sword.

Joshua 6.21

✝

And when Joshua and all Israel saw the ambush had taken the city, and the smoke of the city ascended, they turned again, and slew the men of Ai.

Joshua 8.21

When Israel had made an end of slaying all the inhabitants of Ai in the field, in the wilderness where they chased them, and when they were all fallen on the sword, all the Israelites returned unto Ai, and smote it with the edge of the sword.

Joshua 8.24

✝

And so, all that fell that day, both of men and women, were twelve thousand, all the men of Ai.

Joshua 8.25

✝

For Joshua drew not his spear back until he had utterly destroyed all the inhabitants of Ai.

Joshua 8.26

✝

When they brought those kings unto Joshua, he called all the men of Israel, and said to the captains of the men who went with him, Come near, put your feet upon the necks of these kings. And they came near, and put their feet upon the necks of them.

Joshua 10.24

And Joshua said to them, Fear not, nor be dismayed, be strong and of good courage: for thus shall the Lord do to all your enemies against whom ye fight.

Joshua 10.25

☩

And afterward Joshua smote them, and slew them, and hanged them on five trees: and they were hanging upon the trees until the evening.

Joshua 10.26

☩

So Joshua smote all the country of the hills, and of the south, and of the vale, and of the springs, and all their kings: he left none remaining, but utterly destroyed all that breathed, as the Lord God of Israel commanded.

Joshua 10.40

☩

And when all these kings were met together, they came and pitched together at the waters of Merom, to fight against Israel.

Joshua 11.05

And the Lord said to Joshua, Be not afraid because
of them: for tomorrow about this time will I deliver
them up all slain before Israel: thou shalt hough
their horses, and burn their chariots with fire.

Joshua 11.06

✞

So Joshua came, and all the people of war with
him, against them by the waters of Merom
suddenly; and they fell upon them.

Joshua 11.07

✞

And the Lord delivered them into the hand of
Israel, who smote them, and chased them unto
great Zidon, and unto Misrephothmaim, and unto
the valley of Mizpeh eastward; and they smote
them, until they left them none remaining.

Joshua 11.08

✞

And Joshua did to them as the Lord bade: he houghed
their horses, and burnt their chariots with fire.

Joshua 11.09

And Joshua at that time turned back, and took
Hazor, and smote the king thereof with the sword:
for Hazor was the head of all those kingdoms.

Joshua 11.10

✝

And they smote all the souls therein with the edge
of the sword, utterly destroying them: there was not
any left to breathe: and he burnt Hazor with fire.

Joshua 11.11

✝

And all the cities of those kings, and all the kings of
them, did Joshua take, and smote them with the edge
of the sword, and he utterly destroyed them, as Moses
the servant of the Lord commanded.

Joshua 11.12

✝

And all the spoil of these cities, and the cattle, the
children of Israel took unto themselves; but every
man they smote with the edge of the sword, until they
had destroyed them, neither left they any to breathe.

Joshua 11.14

Joshua made war a long time with all those kings.

Joshua 11.18

✝

So Joshua took the whole land, according to all
that the Lord said unto Moses; and Joshua gave
it for an inheritance unto Israel according to
their divisions by their tribes. And the land
rested from war.

Joshua 11.23

✝

For the Lord hath driven out from before
you great nations and strong: but as for you,
no man hath been able to stand before you
unto this day.

Joshua 23.09

✝

One man of you shall chase a thousand: for
the Lord your God, he it is that fighteth
for you, as he hath promised you.

Joshua 23.10

And he said unto them, Follow after me: for the Lord hath delivered your enemies the Moabites into your hand. And they went down after him, and took the fords of Jordan toward Moab, and suffered not a man to pass over.

Judges 3.28

✝

And they slew of Moab at that time about ten thousand men, all lusty, and all men of valour; and there escaped not a man.

Judges 3.29

✝

So Moab was subdued that day under the hand of Israel. And the land had rest fourscore years.

Judges 3.30

✝

And the angel of the Lord appeared unto him, and said unto him, The Lord is with thee, thou mighty man of valour.

Judges 6.12

And Gideon sent messengers throughout all
Mount Ephraim, saying, come down against
the Midianites, and take before them the waters
unto Bethbarah and Jordan. Then all the men of
Ephraim gathered themselves together, and took
the waters unto Bethbarah and Jordan.

Judges 7.24

✟

And they took two princes of the Midianites,
Oreb and Zeeb; and they slew Oreb upon the
rock Oreb, and Zeeb they slew at the winepress
of Zeeb, and pursued Midian, and brought the
heads of Oreb and Zeeb to Gideon on the
other side of Jordan.

Judges 7.25

✟

And he said unto Jether his firstborn, Up, and
slay them. But the youth drew not his sword:
for he feared, because he was yet a youth.

Judges 8.20

✟

Then Zebah and Zalmunna said, Rise thou, and fall upon us: for as the man is, so is his strength. And Gideon arose, and slew Zebah and Zalmunna, and took away the ornaments that were on their camels' necks.

Judges 8.21

✠

So Jephthah passed over unto the children of Ammon to fight against them; and the Lord delivered them into his hands.

Judges 11.32

✠

And he smote them from Aroer, even till thou come to Minnith, even twenty cities, and unto the plain of the vineyards, with a very great slaughter. Thus the children of Ammon were subdued before the children of Israel.

Judges 11.33

✠

Then the Philistines said, Who hath done this?
And they answered, Samson, the son in law of
the Timnite, because he had taken his wife, and
given her to his companion. And the Philistines
came up, and burnt her and her father with fire.

Judges 15.06

✠

And Samson said unto them, Though ye have
done this, yet will I be avenged of you, and after
that I will cease.

Judges 15.07

✠

He smote them hip and thigh with great slaughter:
then went and dwelt in the top of the rock Etam.

Judges 15.08

✠

. . . the Philistines shouted against him: and the Spirit
of the Lord came mightily upon him, and the cords
upon his arms became as flax that was burnt with
fire, and his bands loosed from off his hands.

Judges 15.14

And he found a new jawbone of an ass, and put forth his hand, and took it, and slew a thousand men therewith.

Judges 15.15

✝

And Samson said, With the jawbone of an ass, heaps upon heaps, with the jaw of an ass have I slain a thousand men.

Judges 15.16

✝

But the children of Benjamin gathered themselves together out of the cities unto Gibeah, to go out to battle against the children of Israel.

Judges 20.14

✝

And the children of Benjamin were numbered at that time out of the cities twenty and six thousand men that drew sword, beside the inhabitants of Gibeah, which were numbered seven hundred chosen men.

Judges 20.15

Among all this people there were seven hundred
chosen men lefthanded; every one could sling
stones at an hair breadth, and not miss.

Judges 20.16

✝

And the men of Israel, beside Benjamin, were
numbered four hundred thousand men that
drew sword: all these were men of war.

Judges 20.17

✝

And the children of Benjamin came forth out of
Gibeah, and destroyed down to the ground of the
Israelites that day twenty and two thousand men.

Judges 20.21

✝

And the people the men of Israel encouraged
themselves, and set their battle again in array
in the place where they put themselves in
array the first day.

Judges 20.22

And the children of Israel wept before the Lord, and asked counsel of the Lord, saying, Shall I go up again to battle against the children of Benjamin my brother? And the Lord said, Go up against him.

Judges 20.23

✝

And the children of Israel came near against the children of Benjamin the second day.

Judges 20.24

✝

And Benjamin went forth against them out of Gibeah the second day, and destroyed down to the ground of the children of Israel again eighteen thousand men; all these drew the sword.

Judges 20.25

✝

And all the men of Israel rose up out of their place, and put themselves in array at Baaltamar: and the liers in wait of Israel came forth out of their places, even out of the meadows of Gibeah.

Judges 20.33

And there came against Gibeah ten thousand chosen men out of all Israel, and the battle was sore: but they knew not that evil was near them.

Judges 20.34

✞

And the Lord smote Benjamin before Israel: and the children of Israel destroyed of the Benjamites that day twenty and five thousand and an hundred men: all these drew the sword.

Judges 20.35

✞

So the children of Benjamin saw that they were smitten: for the men of Israel gave place to the Benjamites, because they trusted unto the liers in wait which they had set beside Gibeah.

Judges 20.36

✞

And the liers in wait hasted, and rushed upon Gibeah; and the liers in wait drew themselves along, and smote all the city with the edge of the sword.

Judges 20.37

Now there was an appointed sign between the men of Israel and the liers in wait, that they should make a great flame with smoke rise up out of the city.

Judges 20.38

✝

And when the men of Israel retired in the battle, Benjamin began to smite and kill of the men of Israel about thirty persons: for they said, Surely they are smitten down before us, as in the first battle.

Judges 20.39

✝

But when the flame began to arise up out of the city with a pillar of smoke, the Benjamites looked behind them, and, behold, the flame of the city ascended up to heaven.

Judges 20.40

✝

And when the men of Israel turned again, the men of Benjamin were amazed: for they saw that evil was come upon them.

Judges 20.41

The Lord killeth, and maketh alive: he bringeth
down to the grave, and bringeth up.

1 Samuel 2.06

✠

The Lord maketh poor, and maketh rich:
he bringeth low, and lifteth up.

1 Samuel 2.07

✠

He raiseth up the poor out of the dust, and
lifteth up the beggar from the dunghill, to set
them among princes, and to make them inherit
the throne of glory: for the pillars of the earth
are the Lord's, and he hath set the world
upon them.

1 Samuel 2.08

✠

He will keep the feet of his saints, and the
wicked shall be silent in darkness; for by
strength shall no man prevail.

1 Samuel 2.09

The adversaries of the Lord shall be broken to pieces; out of heaven shall he thunder upon them: the Lord shall judge the ends of the earth; give strength to his king and exalt his anointed.

1 Samuel 2.10

✠

The word of Samuel came to Israel. Now Israel went against the Philistines to battle, and pitched beside Ebenezer: and the Philistines pitched in Aphek.

1 Samuel 4.01

✠

The Philistines put themselves in array against Israel: when they joined battle, Israel was smitten before the Philistines: and they slew about four thousand men.

1 Samuel 4.02

✠

The elders of Israel said, Why hath the Lord smitten us before the Philistines? Let us fetch the ark of the covenant of the Lord unto us, that, when it cometh, it may save us out of the hand of our enemies.

1 Samuel 4.03

So the people sent to Shiloh, that they might bring from thence the ark of the covenant of the Lord of hosts, and the two sons of Eli, Hophni and Phinehas, were there with the ark of the covenant of God.

1 Samuel 4.04

☦

And when the ark of the covenant of the Lord came into the camp, all Israel shouted with a great shout, so that the earth rang again.

1 Samuel 4.05

☦

And when the Philistines heard the noise, they said, What meaneth the noise of this great shout in the camp of the Hebrews? And they understood that the ark of the Lord was come into the camp.

1 Samuel 4.06

☦

And the Philistines were afraid, for they said, God is come into the camp. And they said, Woe unto us! for there hath not been such a thing heretofore.

1 Samuel 4.07

Woe unto us! who shall deliver us out of the hand
of these mighty Gods? these are the Gods that smote
the Egyptians with all the plagues in the wilderness.

1 Samuel 4.08

✝

Be strong and quit yourselves like men, O Philistines,
that ye be not servants unto the Hebrews, as they have
been to you: quit yourselves like men, and fight.

1 Samuel 4.09

✝

The Philistines fought, and Israel was smitten, and
they fled every man into his tent: and there was a great
slaughter; for there fell of Israel thirty thousand men.

1 Samuel 4.10

✝

And when the Philistines heard that the children of
Israel were gathered together to Mizpeh, the lords
of the Philistines went up against Israel. And
when the children of Israel heard it, they were
afraid of the Philistines.

1 Samuel 7.07

And the children of Israel said to Samuel, Cease not to cry unto the Lord our God for us, that he will save us out of the hand of the Philistines.

1 Samuel 7.08

✠

And Samuel took a sucking lamb, and offered it for a burnt offering wholly unto the Lord: and Samuel cried to the Lord for Israel; and the Lord heard him.

1 Samuel 7.09

✠

And as Samuel was offering up the burnt offering, the Philistines drew near to battle against Israel: but the Lord thundered with a great thunder on that day upon the Philistines, and discomfited them; and they were smitten before Israel.

1 Samuel 7.10

✠

And the men of Israel went out of Mizpeh, and pursued the Philistines, and smote them, until they came under Bethcar.

1 Samuel 7.11

Only fear the Lord, and serve him in truth with all your heart: for consider how great things he hath done for you.

1 Samuel 12.24

✟

But if ye shall still do wickedly, ye shall be consumed, both ye and your king.

1 Samuel 12.25

✟

And Saul and all the people that were with him assembled themselves, and they came to the battle: and, behold, every man's sword was against his fellow, and there was a very great discomfiture.

1 Samuel 14.02

✟

And Saul said to David, Thou art not able to go against this Philistine to fight with him: for thou art but a youth, and he a man of war from his youth.

1 Samuel 17.33

And David said unto Saul, Thy servant kept his father's sheep, and there came a lion, and a bear, and took a lamb out of the flock.

1 Samuel 17.34

✝

And I went after him, and smote him, and delivered it out of his mouth: and when he arose against me, I caught him by his beard, smote him, and slew him.

1 Samuel 17.35

✝

Thy servant slew both the lion and the bear: and this uncircumcised Philistine shall be as one of them, seeing he hath defied the armies of the living God.

1 Samuel 17.36

✝

David said moreover, The Lord that delivered me out of the paw of the lion, and out of the paw of the bear, he will deliver me out of the hand of this Philistine. And Saul said unto David, Go, and the Lord be with thee.

1 Samuel 17.37

And Saul armed David with his armour, and he put
a helmet of brass upon his head; also he armed
him with a coat of mail.

1 Samuel 17.38

✠

And David girded his sword upon his armour, and
he assayed to go; for he had not proved it. And
David said to Saul, I cannot go with these; for I have
not proved them. And David put them off him.

1 Samuel 17.39

✠

And he took his staff in his hand, and chose him
five smooth stones out of the brook, and put them
in a shepherd's bag which he had, even in a scrip;
and his sling was in his hand: and he drew near
to the Philistine.

1 Samuel 17.40

✠

And the Philistine came on and drew near to David;
and the man that bare the shield went before him.

1 Samuel 17.41

And when the Philistine looked about, and saw
David, he disdained him: for he was but a youth,
and ruddy, and of a fair countenance.

1 Samuel 17.42

✝

And the Philistine said unto David, Am I a dog,
that thou comest to me with staves? And the
Philistine cursed David by his gods.

1 Samuel 17.43

✝

And the Philistine said to David, Come to me,
and I will give thy flesh unto the fowls of the air,
and to the beasts of the field.

1 Samuel 17.44

✝

Then said David to the Philistine, Thou comest
to me with a sword, and with a spear, and with
a shield: but I come to thee in the name of the
Lord of hosts, the God of the armies of Israel,
whom thou hast defied.

1 Samuel 17.45

This day will the Lord deliver thee into mine hand; and I will smite thee, and take thine head; and I will give the carcases of the host of the Philistines this day to the fowls of the air, and to the wild beasts of the earth; that all may know that there is a God in Israel.

1 Samuel 17.46

✟

And all this assembly shall know that the Lord saveth not with sword and spear: for the battle is the Lord's, and he will give you into our hands.

1 Samuel 17.47

✟

And it came to pass, when the Philistine came, and drew nigh to meet David, that David hastened, and ran toward the army to meet the Philistine.

1 Samuel 17.48

✟

David put his hand in his bag, and took a stone, and slang it, and smote the Philistine that the stone sunk into his forehead; and he fell on his face to the earth.

1 Samuel 17.49

So David prevailed over the Philistine with a sling
and with a stone, and smote the Philistine, and slew
him; but there was no sword in the hand of David.

1 Samuel 17.50

✟

Therefore David ran, and stood upon the Philistine,
and took his sword, and drew it out of the sheath
thereof, and slew him, and cut off his head therewith.
And when the Philistines saw their champion
was dead, they fled.

1 Samuel 17.51

✟

From the blood of the slain, from the fat of the
mighty, the bow of Jonathan turned not back,
and the sword of Saul returned not empty.

2 Samuel 1.22

✟

Saul and Jonathan were lovely and pleasant in their
lives, and in their death were not divided: they were
swifter than eagles, they were stronger than lions.

2 Samuel 1.23

How are the mighty fallen, and the weapons
of war perished!

2 Samuel 1.27

✞

And David reigned over Israel; and David executed
judgment and justice unto all his people.

2 Samuel 8.15

✞

The God of my rock; in him will I trust: he is
my shield, and the horn of my salvation, my
high tower, and my refuge, my saviour; thou
savest me from violence.

2 Samuel 22.03

✞

I will call on the Lord, who is worthy to be praised:
so shall I be saved from mine enemies.

2 Samuel 22.04

✞

When the waves of death compassed me, the
floods of ungodly men made me afraid.

2 Samuel 22.05

✠

The sorrows of hell compassed me about; the
snares of death prevented me.

2 Samuel 22.06

✠

In my distress I called upon the Lord, and
cried to my God: and he did hear my voice
out of his temple, and my cry did enter
into his ears.

2 Samuel 22.07

✠

The Lord thundered from heaven, and the
most High uttered his voice.

2 Samuel 22.14

✠

And he sent out arrows, and scattered them;
lightning, and discomfited them.

2 Samuel 22.15

✟

And the channels of the sea appeared, the
foundations of the world were discovered,
at the rebuking of the Lord, at the blast of
the breath of his nostrils.

2 Samuel 22.16

✟

He sent from above, he took me; he drew me
out of many waters.

2 Samuel 22.17

✟

He delivered me from my strong enemy,
and from them that hated me: for they
were too strong for me.

2 Samuel 22.18

They prevented me in the day of my calamity:
but the Lord was my stay.

2 Samuel 22.19

✠

He brought me forth also into a large place:
he delivered me, because he delighted in me.

2 Samuel 22.20

✠

The Lord rewarded me according to my
righteousness: according to the cleanness
of my hands hath he recompensed me.

2 Samuel 22.21

✠

For I have kept the ways of the Lord, and have
not wickedly departed from my God.

2 Samuel 22.22

✠

For all his judgments were before me: and as for
his statutes, I did not depart from them.

2 Samuel 22.23

✜

I was also upright before him, and have kept
myself from mine iniquity.

2 Samuel 22.24

✜

Therefore the Lord hath recompensed me according
to my righteousness; according to my cleanness
in his eye sight.

2 Samuel 22.25

✜

The Lord liveth; and blessed be my rock; and
exalted be the God of the rock of my salvation.

2 Samuel 22.47

✜

It is God that avengeth me, and that bringeth
down the people under me.

2 Samuel 22.48

✜

And that bringeth me forth from mine enemies:
thou also hast lifted me up on high above them
that rose up against me: thou hast delivered me
from the violent man.

2 Samuel 22.49

✜

And the young men of the princes of the provinces
went out first; and Benhadad sent out, and they told
him, saying, There are men come out of Samaria.

1 Kings 20.17

✜

And he said, Whether they be come out for peace,
take them alive; or whether they be come out
for war, take them alive.

1 Kings 20.18

So these young men of the princes of the provinces came out of the city, and the army which followed them.

1 Kings 20.19

✟

And they slew every one his man: and the Syrians fled; and Israel pursued them: and Benhadad the king of Syria escaped on an horse with the horsemen.

1 Kings 20.20

✟

And the king of Israel went out, and smote the horses and chariots, and slew the Syrians with a great slaughter.

1 Kings 20.21

✟

And they pitched one over against the other seven days. And so it was, that in the seventh day the battle was joined: and the children of Israel slew of the Syrians an hundred thousand footmen in one day.

1 Kings 20.29

It came to pass that night, that the angel of the Lord went out and smote in the camp of the Assyrians an hundred fourscore and five thousand: and when they arose in the morning, behold, all were dead corpses.

2 Kings 19.35

✠

The sons of Reuben, and the Gadites, and half the tribe of Manasseh, of valiant men able to bear buckler and sword, and shoot with bow, and skilful in war, were four and forty thousand seven hundred and threescore.

1 Chronicles 5.18

✠

And they made war with the Hagarites, with Jetur, and Nephish, and Nodab.

1 Chronicles 5.19

✠

They were helped against them, and the Hagarites were delivered into their hand, and all that were with them: for they cried to God in the battle, and he was intreated of them; because they put their trust in him.

1 Chronicles 5.20

And they took away their cattle; of their camels
fifty thousand, and of sheep two hundred and
fifty thousand, and of asses two thousand,
and of men an hundred thousand.

1 Chronicles 5.21

✜

For there fell down many slain, because the war
was of God. And they dwelt in their steads
until the captivity.

1 Chronicles 5.22

✜

Now the Philistines fought against Israel; and
the men of Israel fled from before the Philistines,
and fell down slain in mount Gilboa.

1 Chronicles 10.01

✜

And the Philistines followed hard after Saul, and after
his sons; and the Philistines slew Jonathan, and
Abinadab, and Malchishua, the sons of Saul.

1 Chronicles 10.02

And the battle went sore against Saul, and the archers hit him, and he was wounded of the archers.

1 Chronicles 10.03

✝

Then said Saul to his armour bearer, Draw thy sword, and thrust me through therewith; lest these uncircumcised come and abuse me. But his armour bearer would not; for he was sore afraid. So Saul took a sword, and fell upon it.

1 Chronicles 10.04

✝

And when his armour bearer saw that Saul was dead, he fell likewise on the sword, and died.

1 Chronicles 10.05

✝

So Saul died, and his three sons, and all his house died together.

1 Chronicles 10.06

And when all the men of Israel that were in the valley saw that they fled, and that Saul and his sons were dead, then they forsook their cities, and fled: and the Philistines came and dwelt in them.

1 Chronicles 10.07

✝

So David waxed greater and greater: for the Lord of hosts was with him.

1 Chronicles 11.09

✝

These also are the chief of the mighty men whom David had, who strengthened themselves with him in his kingdom, and with all Israel, to make him king, according to the word of the Lord concerning Israel.

1 Chronicles 11.10

✝

David met them and said, If ye come peaceably to help, mine heart shall be knit to you: but if ye come to betray me, seeing there is no wrong in mine hands, the God of our fathers look thereon, and rebuke it.

1 Chronicles 12.17

And David consulted with the captains of thousands and hundreds, and with every leader.

1 Chronicles 13.01

✟

And David smote Hadarezer king of Zobah unto Hamath, as he went to stablish his dominion by the river Euphrates.

1 Chronicles 18.03

✟

And David took from him a thousand chariots, and seven thousand horsemen, and twenty thousand footmen: David also houghed all the chariot horses, but reserved of them an hundred chariots.

1 Chronicles 18.04

✟

And when the Syrians of Damascus came to help Hadarezer king of Zobah, David slew of the Syrians two and twenty thousand men.

1 Chronicles 18.05

Thus David the son of Jesse reigned over all Israel.

1 Chronicles 29.26

☦

If thy people go out to war against their enemies by the way that thou shalt send them, and they pray unto thee toward this city which thou hast chosen, and the house which I have built for thy name.

2 Chronicles 6.34

☦

Then hear thou from the heavens their prayer and their supplication, and maintain their cause.

2 Chronicles 6.35

☦

If they sin against thee, (for there is no man which sinneth not,) and thou be angry with them, and deliver them over before their enemies, and they carry them away captives unto a land far off or near.

2 Chronicles 6.36

If they bethink themselves in the land where they are captive, and turn and pray to thee, saying, We have sinned, we have done amiss, and have dealt wickedly.

2 Chronicles 6.37

✞

If they return to thee with their heart and soul in the land of their captivity, where they have carried them captives, and pray toward their land, which thou gave to their fathers, and toward the city which thou chose, and toward the house which I built for thy name.

2 Chronicles 6.38

✞

Then hear thou from the heavens their prayer and their supplications, and maintain their cause, and forgive thy people which have sinned against thee.

2 Chronicles 6.39

✞

Ought ye not to know that the Lord God of Israel gave the kingdom over Israel to David for ever, even to him and to his sons by a covenant of salt?

2 Chronicles 13.05

Yet Jeroboam the son of Nebat, the servant of
Solomon the son of David, is risen up, and hath
rebelled against his lord.

2 Chronicles 13.06

✝

He said, Hearken ye, all Judah, and ye inhabitants
of Jerusalem, and thou king Jehoshaphat, Thus saith
the Lord, Be not afraid nor dismayed by reason of this
great multitude; for the battle is not yours, but God's.

2 Chronicles 20.15

✝

Tomorrow go ye down against them: behold, they
come up by the cliff of Ziz; and ye shall find them at
the end of the brook, before the wilderness of Jeruel.

2 Chronicles 20.16

✝

Ye shall not need to fight in this battle: set yourselves,
stand still, and see the salvation of the Lord, O Judah
and Jerusalem: fear not, nor be dismayed; tomorrow go
out against them: for the Lord will be with you.

2 Chronicles 20.17

And Jehoshaphat bowed his head with his face to the ground: and all Judah and the inhabitants of Jerusalem fell before the Lord, worshipping the Lord.

2 Chronicles 20.18

☩

But if thou wilt go, do it; be strong for the battle: God shall make thee fall before the enemy: for God hath power to help, and to cast down.

2 Chronicles 25.08

☩

Thus the Jews smote all their enemies with the stroke of the sword, and slaughter, and destruction, and did what they would to those that hated them.

Esther 9.05

☩

At destruction and famine thou shalt laugh: neither shalt thou be afraid of the beasts of the earth.

Job 5.22

Behold, God will not cast away a perfect man,
neither will he help the evil doers.

Job 8.20

✝

But man dieth, and wasteth away: yea, man giveth
up the ghost, and where is he?

Job 14.10

✝

So man lieth down, and riseth not: till the heavens
be no more, they shall not awake, nor be raised
out of their sleep.

Job 14.12

✝

For the Lord knoweth the way of the righteous:
but the way of the ungodly shall perish.

Psalms 1.06

✝

Why do the heathen rage, and the people
imagine a vain thing?

Psalms 2.01

✟

Then shall he speak unto them in his wrath, and
vex them in his sore displeasure.

Psalms 2.05

✟

Thou shalt break them with a rod of iron; thou
shalt dash them in pieces like a potter's vessel.

Psalms 2.09

✟

Arise, O Lord; save me, O my God: for thou hast
smitten all mine enemies upon the cheek bone;
thou hast broken the teeth of the ungodly.

Psalms 3.07

✟

Thou shalt destroy them that speak leasing: the Lord will abhor the bloody and deceitful man.

Psalms 5.06

✠

Destroy thou them, O God; let them fall by their own counsels; cast them out in the multitude of their transgressions; for they have rebelled against thee.

Psalms 5.10

✠

But let all those that put their trust in thee rejoice: let them ever shout for joy, because thou defendest them: let them also that love thy name be joyful in thee.

Psalms 5.11

✠

Out of the mouth of babes and sucklings hast thou ordained strength because of thine enemies, that thou mightest still the enemy and the avenger.

Psalms 8.02

When mine enemies are turned back, they shall
fall and perish at thy presence.

Psalms 9.03

✝

The Lord also will be a refuge for the oppressed,
a refuge in times of trouble.

Psalms 9.09

✝

The Lord trieth the righteous: but the wicked and
him that loveth violence his soul hateth.

Psalms 11.05

✝

Upon the wicked he shall rain snares, fire and
brimstone, and an horrible tempest: this shall
be the portion of their cup.

Psalms 11.06

✝

It is God that avengeth me, and subdueth
the people under me.

Psalms 18.47

✝

He delivereth me from mine enemies: yea, thou
liftest me up above those that rise up against me:
thou hast delivered me from the violent man.

Psalms 18.48

✝

The Lord is my shepherd; I shall not want.

Psalms 23.01

✝

He maketh me to lie down in green pastures:
he leadeth me beside the still waters.

Psalms 23.02

✝

He restoreth my soul: he leadeth me in the paths
of righteousness for his name's sake.

Psalms 23.03

✝

Yea, though I walk through the valley of the shadow
of death, I will fear no evil: for thou art with me;
thy rod and thy staff they comfort me.

Psalms 23.04

✝

Thou preparest a table before me in the presence
of mine enemies: thou anointest my head with
oil; my cup runneth over.

Psalms 23.05

✝

Consider mine enemies; for they are many; and
they hate me with cruel hatred.

Psalms 25.19

✝

O keep my soul, and deliver me: let me not be
ashamed; for I put my trust in thee.

Psalms 25.20

✞

The Lord is my light and my salvation; whom
shall I fear? The Lord is the strength of my life;
of whom shall I be afraid?

Psalms 27.01

✞

When the wicked, even mine enemies and
my foes, came upon me to eat up my flesh,
they stumbled and fell.

Psalms 27.02

✞

Though an host should encamp against me,
my heart shall not fear: though war should rise
against me, in this will I be confident.

Psalms 27.03

✞

One thing have I desired of the Lord, that will I seek after; that I may dwell in the house of the Lord all the days of my life, to behold the beauty of the Lord, and to enquire in his temple.

Psalms 27.04

✝

The Lord will give strength unto his people; the Lord will bless his people with peace.

Psalms 29.11

✝

Evil shall slay the wicked: and they that hate the righteous shall be desolate.

Psalms 34.21

✝

Plead my cause, O Lord, with them that strive with me: fight against them that fight against me.

Psalms 35.01

✝

Take hold of shield and buckler, and stand
up for mine help.

Psalms 35.02

✠

Draw out also the spear, and stop the way
against them that persecute me: say unto
my soul, I am thy salvation.

Psalms 35.03

✠

Let them be confounded and put to shame that
seek after my soul: let them be turned back and
brought to confusion that devise my hurt.

Psalms 35.04

✠

Let them be as chaff before the wind: and let
the angel of the Lord chase them.

Psalms 35.05

✠

Let their way be dark and slippery: and let the
angel of the Lord persecute them.

Psalms 35.06

✠

But the meek shall inherit the earth; and shall
delight themselves in the abundance of peace.

Psalms 37.11

✠

The wicked plotteth against the just, and
gnasheth upon him with his teeth.

Psalms 37.12

✠

The Lord shall laugh at him: for he seeth
that his day is coming.

Psalms 37.13

✠

The wicked have drawn out the sword, and have bent their bow, to cast down the poor and needy, and to slay such as be of upright conversation.

Psalms 37.14

✝

Their sword shall enter into their own heart, and their bows shall be broken.

Psalms 37.15

✝

A little that a righteous man hath is better than the riches of many wicked.

Psalms 37.16

✝

For the arms of the wicked shall be broken: but the Lord upholdeth the righteous.

Psalms 37.17

✝

The Lord knoweth the days of the upright: and
their inheritance shall be for ever.

Psalms 37.18

✠

They shall not be ashamed in the evil time: and
in the days of famine they shall be satisfied.

Psalms 37.19

✠

But the wicked shall perish, and the enemies of
the Lord shall be as the fat of lambs: they shall
consume; into smoke shall they consume away.

Psalms 37.20

✠

The wicked borroweth, and payeth not again:
but the righteous sheweth mercy, and giveth.

Psalms 37.21

✠

Gird thy sword upon thy thigh, O most mighty,
with thy glory and thy majesty.

Psalms 45.03

✝

And in thy majesty ride prosperously because of
truth and meekness and righteousness; and thy
right hand shall teach thee terrible things.

Psalms 45.04

✝

Thine arrows are sharp in the heart of the king's
enemies; whereby the people fall under thee.

Psalms 45.05

✝

Destroy, O Lord, and divide their tongues: for
I have seen violence and strife in the city.

Psalms 55.09

✝

Day and night they go about it on the walls thereof:
mischief also and sorrow are in the midst of it.

Psalms 55.10

✠

Wickedness is in the midst thereof: deceit and
guile depart not from her streets.

Psalms 55.11

✠

God shall bless us; and all the ends of the
earth shall fear him.

Psalms 67.07

✠

Let God arise, let his enemies be scattered: let
them also that hate him flee before him.

Psalms 68.01

✠

For, lo, thine enemies, O Lord, for, lo, thine
enemies shall perish; all the workers of iniquity
shall be scattered.

Psalms 92.09

✝

Set thou a wicked man over him: and let Satan
stand at his right hand.

Psalms 109.06

✝

When he shall be judged, let him be condemned:
and let his prayer become sin.

Psalms 109.07

✝

Let his days be few; and let another take his office.

Psalms 109.08

✝

Let his children be fatherless, and his
wife a widow.

Psalms 109.09

✣

Horror hath taken hold upon me because
of the wicked that forsake thy law.

Psalms 119.53

✣

Keep me, O Lord, from the hands of the
wicked; preserve me from the violent man;
who have purposed to overthrow my goings.

Psalms 140.04

✣

For the enemy hath persecuted my soul; he
hath smitten my life down to the ground; he
hath made me to dwell in darkness, as those
that have been long dead.

Psalms 143.03

✣

Deliver me, O Lord, from mine enemies:
I flee unto thee to hide me.

Psalms 143.09

✠

For the upright shall dwell in the land, and
the perfect shall remain in it.

Proverbs 2.21

✠

But the wicked shall be cut off from the earth,
and the transgressors shall be rooted out of it.

Proverbs 2.22

✠

Be not afraid of sudden fear, neither of the
desolation of the wicked, when it cometh.

Proverbs 3.25

✠

The way of the Lord is strength to the upright: but
destruction shall be to the workers of iniquity.

Proverbs 10.29

✟

The righteous shall never be removed: but
the wicked shall not inhabit the earth.

Proverbs 10.30

✟

The integrity of the upright shall guide
them: but the perverseness of transgressors
shall destroy them.

Proverbs 11.03

✟

The evil bow before the good; and the wicked
at the gates of the righteous.

Proverbs 14.19

✟

It is an abomination to kings to commit wickedness:
for the throne is established by righteousness.

Proverbs 16.12

✝

Pride goeth before destruction, and an
haughty spirit before a fall.

Proverbs 16.18

✝

The glory of young men is their strength: and
the beauty of old men is the grey head.

Proverbs 20.29

✝

If thine enemy be hungry, give him bread
to eat; and if he be thirsty, give him
water to drink.

Proverbs 25.21

✝

A whip for the horse, a bridle for the ass,
and a rod for the fool's back.

Proverbs 26.03

✛

Faithful are the wounds of a friend; but the
kisses of an enemy are deceitful.

Proverbs 27.06

✛

A prudent man foreseeth the evil, and
hideth himself; but the simple pass on,
and are punished.

Proverbs 27.12

✛

Whoso walketh uprightly shall be saved:
but he that is perverse in his ways
shall fall at once.

Proverbs 28.18

✛

When the righteous are in authority, the people rejoice: but when the wicked beareth rule, the people mourn.

Proverbs 29.02

✝

When the wicked are multiplied, transgression increaseth: but the righteous shall see their fall.

Proverbs 29.16

✝

A time to kill, and a time to heal; a time to break down, and a time to build up.

Ecclesiastes 3.03

✝

A time to love, and a time to hate; a time of war, and a time of peace.

Ecclesiastes 3.08

✝

All hold swords, being expert in war: every man hath his sword upon his thigh because of fear in the night.

Song of Solomon 3.08

✠

Their roaring shall be like a lion, they shall roar like young lions: yea, they shall roar, and lay hold of the prey, and carry it away safe, and none shall deliver it.

Isaiah 5.29

✠

And I will punish the world for their evil, and the wicked for their iniquity; and I will cause the arrogancy of the proud to cease, and will lay low the haughtiness of the terrible.

Isaiah 13.11

✠

Then the angel of the Lord went forth, and smote in the camp of the Assyrians a hundred and fourscore and five thousand: and when they arose early in the morning, behold, they were all dead corpses.

Isaiah 37.36

For, behold, the darkness shall cover the earth, and gross darkness the people: but the Lord shall arise upon thee, and his glory shall be seen upon thee.

Isaiah 60.02

✝

For, behold, the Lord will come with fire, and with his chariots like a whirlwind, to render his anger with fury, and his rebuke with flames of fire.

Isaiah 66.15

✝

For by fire and by his sword will the Lord plead with all flesh: and the slain of the Lord shall be many.

Isaiah 66.16

✝

Prepare ye war against her; arise, and let us go up at noon. Woe unto us! for the day goeth away, for the shadows of the evening are stretched out.

Jeremiah 6.04

✝

Arise, and let us go by night, and let us destroy her palaces.

Jeremiah 6.05

✠

Hear, O earth: behold, I will bring evil upon this people, even the fruit of their thoughts, because they have not hearkened unto my words, nor to my law, but rejected it.

Jeremiah 6.19

✠

They shall lay hold on bow and spear; they are cruel, and have no mercy; their voice roareth like the sea; and they ride upon horses, set in array as men for war against thee, O daughter of Zion.

Jeremiah 6.23

✠

And I will dash them one against another, even the fathers and sons together, saith the Lord: I will not pity, nor spare, nor have mercy, but destroy them.

Jeremiah 13.14

Order ye the buckler and shield,
and draw near to battle.

Jeremiah 46.03

✠

Harness the horses; and get up, ye horsemen, and
stand forth with your helmets; furbish the spears,
and put on the brigandines.

Jeremiah 46.04

✠

Come up, ye horses; and rage, ye chariots; and let the
mighty men come forth; the Ethiopians and the Liby-
ans, that handle the shield; and the Lydians, that handle
and bend the bow.

Jeremiah 46.09

✠

For this is the day of the Lord God of hosts, a day of
vengeance, that he may avenge him of his adversaries:
and the sword shall devour, and it shall be satiate and
made drunk with their blood . . .

Jeremiah 46.10

The Lord hath opened his armoury, and hath brought forth the weapons of his indignation: for this is the work of the Lord God of hosts in the land of the Chaldeans.

Jeremiah 50.25

✝

Come against her from the utmost border, open her storehouses: cast her up as heaps, and destroy her utterly: let nothing of her be left.

Jeremiah 50.26

✝

Slay all her bullocks; let them go down to the slaughter: woe unto them! for their day is come, the time of their visitation.

Jeremiah 50.27

✝

A sword is upon the Chaldeans, saith the Lord, and upon the inhabitants of Babylon, and upon her princes, and upon her wise men.

Jeremiah 50.35

A sword is upon the liars; and they shall dote: a sword is upon her mighty men; and they shall be dismayed.

Jeremiah 50.36

✠

A sword is upon their horses, and upon their chariots, and upon all the mingled people that are in the midst of her; and they shall become as women: a sword is upon her treasures; and they shall be robbed.

Jeremiah 50.37

✠

Thou art my battle axe and weapons of war: for with thee will I break in pieces the nations, and with thee will I destroy kingdoms.

Jeremiah 51.20

✠

And with thee will I break in pieces the horse and his rider; and with thee will I break in pieces the chariot and his rider.

Jeremiah 51.21

With thee also will I break in pieces man and
woman; and with thee will I break in pieces old
and young; and with thee will I break in pieces
the young man and the maid.

Jeremiah 51.22

✠

I will also break in pieces with thee the shepherd
and his flock; and with thee will I break in pieces
the husbandman and his yoke of oxen; and with
thee will I break in pieces captains and rulers.

Jeremiah 51.23

✠

And I will render unto Babylon and to all the
inhabitants of Chaldea all their evil that they have
done in Zion in your sight, saith the Lord.

Jeremiah 51.24

✠

They that be slain with the sword are better than
they that be slain with hunger: for these pine away,
stricken through for want of the fruits of the field.

Lamentations 4.09

The cities shall be laid waste; the high places shall be desolate; your altars laid waste and made desolate, and your idols be broken and cease, and your images may be cut down, and your works be abolished.

Ezekiel 6.06

✝

And the slain shall fall in the midst of you, and ye shall know that I am the Lord.

Ezekiel 6.07

✝

Yet will I leave a remnant, that ye may have some that shall escape the sword among the nations, when ye shall be scattered through the countries.

Ezekiel 6.08

✝

They that escape shall remember me . . . because I am broken with their whorish heart, which hath departed from me, and their eyes, which go a whoring after their idols: and they shall lothe themselves for the evils they have committed in their abominations.

Ezekiel 6.09

Make a chain: for the land is full of bloody
crimes, and the city is full of violence.

Ezekiel 7.23

✞

Ye have feared the sword; and I will bring
a sword upon you, saith the Lord God.

Ezekiel 11.08

✞

And I will bring you out of the midst thereof,
and deliver you into the hands of strangers,
and will execute judgments among you.

Ezekiel 11.09

✞

Ye shall fall by the sword; I will judge you
in the border of Israel; and ye shall know
that I am the Lord.

Ezekiel 11.10

✞

This city shall not be your caldron, neither shall
ye be the flesh in the midst thereof; but I will
judge you in the border of Israel.

Ezekiel 11.11

✝

By the swords of the mighty will I cause thy multitude
to fall . . . all of them: and they shall spoil the pomp of
Egypt, and the multitude thereof shall be destroyed.

Ezekiel 32.12

✝

Say unto them, As I live, saith the Lord God, I have no
pleasure in the death of the wicked; but that the wicked
turn from his way and live: turn ye, turn ye from your
evil ways; for why will ye die, O house of Israel?

Ezekiel 33.11

✝

Thus saith the Lord . . . surely they in the wastes
shall fall by the sword, and him in the open field will
I give to the beasts to be devoured, and they in the
forts and in the caves shall die of the pestilence.

Ezekiel 33.27

For I will lay the land most desolate, and the pomp of her strength shall cease; and the mountains of Israel shall be desolate, that none shall pass through.

Ezekiel 33.28

✝

Then shall they know that I am the Lord, when I have laid the land most desolate because of all their abominations which they have committed.

Ezekiel 33.29

✝

I will lay thy cities waste, and thou shalt be desolate, and thou shalt know that I am the Lord.

Ezekiel 35.04

✝

Thou, O king, art a king of kings: for the God of heaven hath given thee a kingdom, power, and strength, and glory.

Daniel 2.37

✝

And whoso falleth not down and worshippeth
shall the same hour be cast into the midst of
a burning fiery furnace.

Daniel 3.06

✝

Woe unto them! for they have fled from me:
destruction unto them! because they have
transgressed against me: though I have redeemed
them, yet they have spoken lies against me.

Hosea 7.13

✝

I will meet them as a bear that is bereaved
of her whelps, and will rend the caul of their
heart, and there will I devour them like a lion:
the wild beast shall tear them.

Hosea 13.08

✝

Fear not, O land; be glad and rejoice: for the
Lord will do great things.

Joel 2.21

Proclaim ye this among the Gentiles; Prepare war, wake up the mighty men, let all the men of war draw near; let them come up.

Joel 3.09

✠

Beat your plowshares into swords and your pruning hooks into spears: let the weak say, I am strong.

Joel 3.10

✠

Assemble yourselves, and come, all ye heathen, and gather yourselves together round about: thither cause thy mighty ones to come down, O Lord.

Joel 3.11

✠

Let the heathen be wakened, and come up to the valley of Jehoshaphat: for there will I sit to judge all the heathen round about.

Joel 3.12

✠

I have sent among you pestilence . . . your young men have I slain with the sword . . . I have made the stink of your camps to come up unto your nostrils: yet have ye not returned unto me, saith the Lord.

Amos 4.10

✝

I have overthrown some of you, as God overthrew Sodom and Gomorrah, and ye were as a firebrand plucked out of the burning: yet have ye not returned unto me, saith the Lord.

Amos 4.11

✝

Though thou exalt thyself as the eagle, and though thou set thy nest among the stars, thence will I bring thee down, saith the Lord.

Obadiah 1.04

✝

For the day of the Lord is near upon all the heathen: as thou hast done, it shall be done unto thee: thy reward shall return upon thine own head.

Obadiah 1.15

Thine hand shall be lifted up upon thine adversaries,
and all thine enemies shall be cut off.

Micah 5.09

☩

And it shall come to pass in that day, saith the
Lord, that I will cut off thy horses out of the
midst of thee, and I will destroy thy chariots.

Micah 5.10

☩

And I will cut off the cities of thy land,
and throw down all thy strong holds.

Micah 5.11

☩

And I will cut off witchcrafts out of thine hand;
and thou shalt have no more soothsayers.

Micah 5.12

☩

Thy graven images also will I cut off, and thy standing images out of the midst of thee; and thou shalt no more worship the work of thine hands.

Micah 5.13

✝

And I will pluck up thy groves out of the midst of thee: so will I destroy thy cities.

Micah 5.14

✝

And I will execute vengeance in anger and fury upon the heathen, such as they have not heard.

Micah 5.15

✝

God is jealous, and the Lord revengeth; the Lord revengeth, and is furious; the Lord will take vengeance on his adversaries, and he reserveth wrath for his enemies.

Nahum 1.02

The Lord is slow to anger, and great in power, and
will not at all acquit the wicked: the Lord hath his
way in the whirlwind and in the storm, and the
clouds are the dust of his feet.

Nahum 1.03

✝

The Lord is good, a strong hold in the day of trouble;
and he knoweth them that trust in him.

Nahum 1.07

✝

But with an overrunning flood he will make an
utter end of the place thereof, and darkness
shall pursue his enemies.

Nahum 1.08

✝

Woe to the bloody city! it is all full of lies and
robbery; the prey departeth not.

Nahum 3.01

✝

The noise of a whip, the noise of the rattling wheels, the prancing horses, and the jumping chariots.

Nahum 3.02

✝

The horseman lifteth up both the bright sword and the glittering spear: and there is a multitude of slain, and a great number of carcases; there is none end of their corpses; they stumble upon their corpses.

Nahum 3.03

✝

And I will bring distress upon men, that they shall walk like blind men, because they have sinned against the Lord: and their blood shall be poured out as dust, and their flesh as the dung.

Zephaniah 1.17

✝

I will overthrow kingdoms, and I will destroy the heathen; and I will overthrow the chariots, and those that ride in them; and the horses and their riders shall come down, every one by the sword of his brother.

Haggai 2.22

And if thy right eye offend thee, pluck it out, and cast it from thee: for it is profitable for thee that one of thy members should perish, and not that thy whole body should be cast into hell.

Matthew 5.29

✝

And if thy right hand offend thee, cut it off, and cast it from thee: for it is profitable for thee that one of thy members should perish, and not that thy whole body should be cast into hell.

Matthew 5.30

✝

Ye have heard that it hath been said, An eye for an eye, and a tooth for a tooth.

Matthew 5.38

✝

Beware of false prophets, which come to you in sheep's clothing, but inwardly they are ravening wolves.

Matthew 7.15

The Son of man shall send forth his angels, and they shall gather out of his kingdom all things that offend, and them which do iniquity.

Matthew 13.41

✝

And shall cast them into a furnace of fire: there shall be wailing and gnashing of teeth.

Matthew 13.42

✝

Then shall the righteous shine forth as the sun in the kingdom of their Father. Who hath ears to hear, let him hear.

Matthew 13.43

✝

For many are called, but few are chosen.

Matthew 22.14

✝

Ye serpents, ye generation of vipers, how can
ye escape the damnation of hell?

Matthew 23.33

✝

And Jesus answered and said unto them, Take
heed that no man deceive you.

Matthew 24.04

✝

For many shall come in my name, saying,
I am Christ; and shall deceive many.

Matthew 24.05

✝

And ye shall hear of wars and rumours of wars:
see that ye be not troubled: for all these things
must come to pass, but the end is not yet.

Matthew 24.06

✝

For nation shall rise against nation, and kingdom against kingdom: and there shall be famines, and pestilences, and earthquakes, in divers places.

Matthew 24.07

✝

All these are the beginning of sorrows.

Matthew 24.08

✝

For whosoever will save his life shall lose it: but whosoever will lose his life for my sake, the same shall save it.

Luke 9.24

✝

He that is not with me is against me: and he that gathereth not with me scattereth.

Luke 11.23

✝

No servant can serve two masters: for either he will hate the one, and love the other; or else he will hold to the one, and despise the other. Ye cannot serve God and mammon.

Luke 16.13

✝

I am the good shepherd, and know my sheep, and am known of mine.

John 10.14

✝

As the Father knoweth me, even so know I the Father: and I lay down my life for the sheep.

John 10.15

✝

He that hateth me hateth my Father also.

John 15.23

✝

For this cause God gave them up unto vile affections:
for even their women did change the natural use
into that which is against nature.

Romans 1.26

✜

And likewise also the men, leaving the natural
use of the woman, burned in their lust one toward
another; men with men working that which is
unseemly, and receiving in themselves that
recompence of their error which was meet.

Romans 1.27

✜

And even as they did not like to retain God in their
knowledge, God gave them over to a reprobate
mind, to do those things which are not convenient.

Romans 1.28

✜

Being filled with all unrighteousness, fornication,
wickedness, covetousness, maliciousness; full of
envy, murder, debate, deceit, malignity; whisperers,

Romans 1.29

Backbiters, haters of God, despiteful, proud, boasters, inventors of evil things, disobedient to parents,

Romans 1.30

✝

Without understanding, covenant breakers, without natural affection, implacable, unmerciful.

Romans 1.31

✝

Who knowing the judgment of God, that they which commit such things are worthy of death, not only do the same, but have pleasure in them that do them.

Romans 1.32

✝

Therefore thou art inexcusable, O man, whosoever thou art that judgest: for wherein thou judgest another, thou condemnest thyself; for thou that judgest doest the same things.

Romans 2.01

✝

For the wages of sin is death; but the gift of God is eternal life through Jesus Christ our Lord.

Romans 6.23

✤

As it is written, For thy sake we are killed all the day long; we are accounted as sheep for the slaughter.

Romans 8.36

✤

For the kingdom of God is not in word, but in power.

1 Corinthians 4.20

✤

When I was a child, I spake as a child, I understood as a child, I thought as a child: but when I became a man, I put away childish things.

1 Corinthians 13.11

✤

For now we see through a glass, darkly; but then
face to face: now I know in part; but then shall
I know even as also I am known.

1 Corinthians 13.12

✠

For he must reign, till he hath put all
enemies under his feet.

1 Corinthians 15.25

✠

The last enemy that shall be destroyed is death.

1 Corinthians 15.26

✠

If after the manner of men I have fought with
beasts at Ephesus, what advantageth it me,
if the dead rise not? let us eat and drink;
for tomorrow we die.

1 Corinthians 15.32

✠

Be not deceived: evil communications
corrupt good manners.

1 Corinthians 15.33

✠

O death, where is thy sting? O grave,
where is thy victory?

1 Corinthians 15.55

✠

The sting of death is sin; and the strength
of sin is the law.

1 Corinthians 15.56

✠

But thanks be to God, which giveth us the
victory through our Lord Jesus Christ.

1 Corinthians 15.57

✠

Watch ye, stand fast in the faith,
quit you like men, be strong.

1 Corinthians 16.13

✝

Persecuted, but not forsaken; cast down,
but not destroyed.

2 Corinthians 4.09

✝

But if ye bite and devour one another,
take heed that ye be not consumed
one of another.

Galatians 5.15

✝

If we live in the Spirit, let us
also walk in the Spirit.

Galatians 5.25

✝

Let us not be desirous of vain glory, provoking
one another, envying one another.

Galatians 5.26

✠

Be ye angry, and sin not: let not the sun go
down upon your wrath.

Ephesians 4.26

✠

Neither give place to the devil.

Ephesians 4.27

✠

Finally, my brethren, be strong in the Lord,
and in the power of his might.

Ephesians 6.10

✠

Put on the whole armour of God, that ye may be
able to stand against the wiles of the devil.

Ephesians 6.11

✝

For we wrestle not against flesh and blood, but
against principalities, against powers, against the
rulers of the darkness of this world, against
spiritual wickedness in high places.

Ephesians 6.12

✝

Above all, taking the shield of faith, wherewith
ye shall be able to quench all the fiery darts
of the wicked.

Ephesians 6.16

✝

And take the helmet of salvation, and the sword
of the Spirit, which is the word of God.

Ephesians 6.17

✝

When Christ, who is our life, shall appear, then shall ye also appear with him in glory.

Colossians 3.04

✞

For ye are our glory and joy.

1 Thessalonians 2.02

✞

For yourselves know perfectly that the day of the Lord so cometh as a thief in the night.

1 Thessalonians 5.02

✞

Drink no longer water, but use a little wine for thy stomach's sake and thine often infirmities.

1 Timothy 5.23

✞

For we brought nothing into this world, and it
is certain we can carry nothing out.

1 Timothy 6.07

✝

Fight the good fight of faith, lay hold on eternal life,
whereunto thou art also called, and hast professed a
good profession before many witnesses.

1 Timothy 6.12

✝

I have fought a good fight, I have finished
my course, I have kept the faith.

2 Timothy 4.07

✝

Henceforth there is laid up for me a crown of
righteousness, which the Lord, the righteous judge,
shall give me at that day: and not to me only, but
unto all them also that love his appearing.

2 Timothy 4.08

✝

Unto the pure all things are pure: but unto them that are defiled and unbelieving is nothing pure; but even their mind and conscience is defiled.

Titus 1.15

✝

For our God is a consuming fire.

Hebrews 12.29

✝

From whence come wars and fightings among you? come they not hence, even of your lusts that war in your members?

James 4.01

✝

Ye lust, and have not: ye kill, and desire to have, and cannot obtain: ye fight and war, yet ye have not, because ye ask not.

James 4.02

✝

Ye ask, and receive not, because ye ask amiss, that ye may consume it upon your lusts.

James 4.03

✠

Speak not evil one of another, brethren. He that speaketh evil of his brother, and judgeth his brother, speaketh evil of the law, and judgeth the law: but if thou judge the law, thou art not a doer of the law, but a judge.

James 4.11

✠

There is one lawgiver, who is able to save and to destroy: who art thou that judgest another?

James 4.12

✠

Little children, it is the last time: and as ye have heard that antichrist shall come, even now are there many antichrists; whereby we know that it is the last time.

1 John 2.18

He that committeth sin is of the devil; for the devil sinneth from the beginning. For this purpose the Son of God was manifested, that he might destroy the works of the devil.

1 John 3.08

✠

Marvel not, my brethren, if the world hate you.

1 John 3.13

✠

We know that we have passed from death unto life, because we love the brethren. He that loveth not his brother abideth in death.

1 John 3.14

✠

And we know that we are of God, and the whole world lieth in wickedness.

1 John 5.19

✠

Little children, keep yourselves from idols. Amen.

1 John 5.21

✠

And he that overcometh, and keepeth my
works unto the end, to him will I give power
over the nations.

Revelation 2.26

✠

And in those days shall men seek death, and
shall not find it; and shall desire to die, and
death shall flee from them.

Revelation 9.06

✠

And the seventh angel sounded; and there were
great voices in heaven, saying, The kingdoms
of this world are become the kingdoms of
our Lord, and of his Christ; and he shall
reign for ever and ever.

Revelation 11.15

Let him that hath understanding count the number of the beast: for it is the number of a man; and his number is six hundred threescore and six.

Revelation 13.18

✝

And I saw an angel come down from heaven, having the key of the bottomless pit and a great chain in his hand.

Revelation 20.01

✝

And he laid hold on the dragon, that old serpent, which is the Devil, and Satan, and bound him a thousand years.

Revelation 20.02

✝

And cast him into the bottomless pit, and shut him up, and set a seal upon him, that he should deceive the nations no more, till the thousand years should be fulfilled: and after that he must be loosed a little season.

Revelation 20.03

And when the thousand years are expired, Satan
shall be loosed out of his prison,

Revelation 20.07

✠

And shall go out to deceive the nations which
are in the four quarters of the earth, Gog,
and Magog, to gather them together to battle:
the number of whom is as the sand of the sea.

Revelation 20.08

✠

The grace of our Lord Jesus Christ be
with you all. Amen.

Revelation 22.21

✠

www.ingramcontent.com/pod-product-compliance
Lightning Source LLC
Chambersburg PA
CBHW021129020426
42331CB00005B/681